VIVA! LATINO CELEBRATIONS
CELEBRATING CARNIVAL!

MARISA ORGULLO

PowerKiDS press
New York

Published in 2019 by The Rosen Publishing Group, Inc.
29 East 21st Street, New York, NY 10010

Copyright © 2019 by The Rosen Publishing Group, Inc.

All rights reserved. No part of this book may be reproduced in any form without permission in writing from the publisher, except by a reviewer.

First Edition

Editor: Brianna Battista
Book Design: Reann Nye

Photo Credits: Cover (child) Ingrid Firmhofer/Alamy.com; cover (background) CP DC Press/Shutterstock.com; p. 5 MAURO PIMENTEL/AFP/Getty Images; p. 7 Tomi Mika/Shutterstock.com; p. 9 Val Thoermer/Shutterstock.com; pp. 11, 13 CARL DE SOUZA/AFP/Getty Images; p. 15 OMAR TORRES/AFP/Getty Images; pp. 17, 19 Sean Drakes/LatinContent Editorial/Getty Images; p. 21 Skip Bolen/Getty Images Entertainment/Getty Images; p. 22 Dave King/Dorling Kindersley/Getty Images.

Library of Congress Cataloging-in-Publication Data

Names: Orgullo, Marisa, author.
Title: Celebrating carnival! / Marisa Orgullo.
Description: New York : PowerKids Press, [2019] | Series: Viva! Latino
  celebrations | Includes index.
Identifiers: LCCN 2018020446| ISBN 9781538342060 (library bound) | ISBN
  9781538342046 (pbk.) | ISBN 9781538342053 (6 pack)
Subjects: LCSH: Carnival-Latin America-Juvenile literature. |
  Carnival-Caribbean Area-Juvenile literature.
Classification: LCC GT4213.5 .O74 2019 | DDC 394.2698-dc23
LC record available at https://lccn.loc.gov/2018020446

CPSIA Compliance Information: Batch #CWPK19: For Further Information contact Rosen Publishing, New York, New York at 1-800-237-9932

CONTENTS

What Is Carnival?............. 4
Brazil and Mexico 10
Caribbean Islands 16
Glossary..................... 23
Index 24
Websites 24

What Is Carnival?

Carnival is a special time in Latin America. Here, this holiday most often happens in February or March. It's a big party in honor of life! People dress up and go to lively parties and colorful parades. It's **celebrated** throughout the world, but some of the best-known Carnivals happen in Latin America.

Brazil's Carnival, shown here, welcomes many thousands of visitors from all over the world each year.

Carnival has been celebrated for hundreds of years. It has **roots** in many places, but it's famously a holiday in preparation for Lent. Lent is the 40 days before Easter when practicing **Catholics** give up things they enjoy. Carnival helps people get together and have fun before they give up things they like for a few weeks.

Carnival is also a big celebration in many European cities. These festival-goers are in Venice, Italy.

When Carnival spread to Latin America, different areas and groups put their own spin on the celebrations. In most places, Carnival starts on a weekend and stops on Shrove Tuesday, the last day before Lent. The parties and celebrations are different in each country, but they all have some things in common.

No matter where a person celebrates Carnival, there will be music and dancing!

Brazil and Mexico

Rio de Janeiro has the most well-known Carnival celebration. Many people visit from out of town to join the party. Parade marchers walk and dance to wild beats in the street. At night, people go to masked balls. They dress up as superheroes, princesses, devils, and animals. The **costumes** are beautiful!

At Carnival, many of the costumes are homemade with objects such as feathers and beads.

Rio's Carnival is also famous for a special type of music and dance. Brazilians young and old take part in dance groups called samba schools. Samba is a type of music and dance with European and African roots. During Carnival, samba schools dance in parades alongside **floats** of all shapes and sizes.

The Carnival in Rio has gotten so large that the government built a big building where all the guests can watch the dancers. The streets were too crowded!

In Mexico, seaside cities such as Mazatlán and Veracruz have their own Carnival practices. Children make cascarones (kas-kah-ROH-nays), or eggshells filled with **confetti**. The children then break them for good luck. On the streets, people laugh at clowns and jugglers. Fireworks light up the sky. The parties are smaller than Rio's, but they're full of joy!

In some of Mexico's Carnival celebrations, you'll find Chinelo dancers instead of samba dancers.

Caribbean Islands

Trinidad and Tobago is a country made up of two islands in the Caribbean. The people there celebrate Carnival by forming teams called bands. People play and sing a type of music called calypso (kuh-LIP-soh), and drummers pound on steel pans. The bands' members wear costumes, and they dance together in the streets.

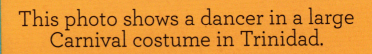
This photo shows a dancer in a large Carnival costume in Trinidad.

Even the children of Trinidad and Tobago form bands during Carnival. Girls and boys dress in costumes that look like butterflies, flowers, knights on horses, or even jellyfish. Some costumes are so big that they must be rolled on wheels as the children walk! Both adults and children can have fun at Carnival.

Boys and girls often dress up and take part in the parades, too!

Carnival isn't only celebrated in Latin America. Some Americans celebrate, too. In New Orleans, Louisiana, the main part of the celebration is Mardi Gras (MAHR-dee GRAH). Parades with flashy floats crowd the streets. Costumed riders throw strings of colorful beads to visitors. New Orleans's Carnival has a king called Rex. He rules the party!

Mardi Gras has a Rex parade every year. It's one of the most popular parts of the celebration.

Carnival is an important and wonderful part of life in many countries. It's an event that brings joy to people in many countries as they celebrate everything that they enjoy in life. People from Latin America and all over the world come together to celebrate. The Carnival party is open to everyone!

GLOSSARY

Catholic: A member of the Roman Catholic church.

celebrate: To honor an important moment by doing special things.

confetti: Very small pieces of colored paper.

costumes: Clothes that make a person look like someone or something else.

float: A car or truck used to present art and performances in a parade.

root: The cause of something.

INDEX

B
Brazil, 4

C
calypso, 16
Caribbean, 16
cascarones, 14
Catholics, 6
Chinelo dancers, 14

E
Easter, 6

F
February, 4

I
Italy, 6

L
Latin America, 4, 8, 20, 22
Lent, 6, 8
Louisiana, 20

M
March, 4
Mardi Gras, 20
Mazatlán, 14
Mexico, 14

N
New Orleans, 20

R
Rex, 20
Rio de Janeiro, 10, 12, 14

S
samba schools, 12
Shrove Tuesday, 8

T
Trinidad and Tobago, 16, 18

V
Venice, 6
Veracruz, 14

WEBSITES

Due to the changing nature of Internet links, PowerKids Press has developed an online list of websites related to the subject of this book. This site is updated regularly. Please use this link to access the list: www.powerkidslinks.com/lcila/carnival